From eGovernment to mGovernment: Facing the Inevitable

IBRAHIM KUSHCHU

M HALID KUSCU

mobileGov UK series on mGovernment

Vol I

IBRAHIM KUSHCHU and M HALID KUSCU

ISBN-13: 978-1912037001

ISBN-10: 1912037009

DEDICATION

To all those who believe in the power of sharing knowledge …

ACKNOWLEDGMENTS

The field of mobileGovernment as a practice has been growing significantly and implemented successfully by various governments since our early efforts from early 200s by valuable contributions of my students in Japan, colleagues and many professionals from all around the world, all of whom, deserve gratitude and appreciation. Thanks to all wholeheartedly. Special thanks to the team at the mGovLab Japan and mobileGov UK.

Abstract:

The changes in the Internet and World Wide Web technologies and services lead to new developments in the way e-government efforts provide services to citizens and businesses, and in the way governments handles their internal operations. One of the revolutionary developments comes from adoption of wireless mobile technologies in government related activities: m-government. In this paper we present technological drivers of m-government and present cases where these technologies are being used. The paper concludes with discussions of challenges for m-government implementations now and in the future.

Keywords: Mobile Government, e-Government

IBRAHIM KUSHCHU and M HALID KUSCU

1. Introduction

Advances in E-government oriented technologies and services are taking place with a considerable speed around the world. E-government efforts aim to benefit from the use of most innovative forms of information technologies, particularly web-based Internet applications, in improving governments' fundamental functions. These functions are now spreading the use of mobile and wireless technologies and creating a new direction: mobile government (m-government).

Despite its early stage, m-government seems to have a substantial influence on the generation of set of complex strategies and tools for e-government efforts and on their roles and functions. M-government is inevitable. The number of people having access to mobile phones and mobile internet connection is increasing rapidly. The mobile access - anywhere any time – is becoming a natural part of daily life, and the governments will have to transform their activities according to this demand of convenience and efficiency of interactions for all parties.

The coming age of m-government raises several interesting questions. Will m-government replace the e-government activities? Despite its significance m-government cannot be seen as replacing e-government and in many cases it will be complementary to e-government efforts. The conventional e-government efforts provide services through wired network with interactive and relatively intelligent web applications. The value of m-government comes from the capabilities of applications supporting mobility of the citizens, businesses and internal operations of the governments. For example, supporting law enforcement agents who are on patrol is a distinctive advantage of mobile government services over conventional e-government implementations. Wireless applications may enable greater mobilization of the government officials with ability to handle real-time information concerning, for example, crimes, accidents, safety and other public issues.

The synergy between e-government and m-government may be of concern especially for those countries that are already gone ahead in making substantial investments in e-government implementations. Now that m-government is inevitable, extending activities to wireless devices and networks will enable these countries to be more proactive in their operations and services by providing real-time and up-to-date information to the officials on the move and by offering citizens a broader selection of choices of interaction. For these countries, m-government implementations are emerging as one of the additional value-added features for the integrated and flexible data communication and exchange mechanism among government units. They may use more advanced wireless applications such as location-based information exchanges. These emerging applications are expected to stimulate m-government by enhancing location-based services such as fire fighting and medical emergencies. If requested, these technologies may be used to transfer location-specific information to mobile device users (i.e., information about traffic conditions or the weather).

How about the implications for those countries that have not yet started or are at the early stages of e-government strategy and implementation processes? These countries may have more advantages depending on type of the issues faced by the governments. In developing countries mobile government applications may become a key method for reaching citizens and promoting exchange of communications especially when used in remote areas. In such countries with insufficient conventional telecom infrastructures and greater acceptance of mobile phones, ability of reaching rural areas may be considered as an important feature of m-government.

As this brief discussion suggests, m-government is in its early stage of development. It may be defined as a *strategy and its implementation involving the utilization of all kinds of wireless and mobile technology, services, applications and devices for improving benefits to the parties involved in e-government including citizens, businesses and all government units.* The developments in e-business and m-business areas are influencing mobile technology adoption by governments. In parallel, the existing research in m-government field often focuses a few applications (Easton 2002) and mobile business issues as they relate to e-government (Holmes 2001). There is now a growing need to examine m-government related issues from the perspectives of their own and build a framework for the study of m-government efforts.

In this paper, we would like take a technology-based view of challenges and future developments of m-government. We start by briefly visiting the evolution of Internet and the World Wide Web from wired to wireless technologies. We will next present various cases where these new mobile technologies are used for m-government implementations. We will then evaluate advances in m-government efforts in terms of at least four important challenges. These include issues related to developing necessary infrastructure; level of mobile Internet penetration and accessibility; legal issues; and, privacy and security. Finally we conclude with a discussion, which may help practitioners and policy makers in distinguishing between e-government and m-government provisions and realizing the importance of synergy between the two.

2. The Drivers of M-government

The forces influencing the move from e-government to m-government activities include major changes in the technological infrastructure and the advances in mobile telecommunication services. The technological changes can be broadly described under three major trends: mobile device penetration; convergence of wired Internet and wireless telecommunication networks; and the move towards 3G services and higher data transfer rates. The services include personalisation, location based services and context aware applications. In the following sections we would like to visit each of these important factors, which form a strong foundations for the governments to build their mobile services.

2.1 Mobile Device Penetration

Mobile devices are now taking significant roles in our daily and business life. At the end of year 2001, approximately 14% of the world population – 850 Million people were mobile phone users This growth has been spectacular especially in Europe after the telecom industry de-regulation and adoption of Global System for Mobile (GSM) communications (Sadeh, 2002). Now, mobile phones are no longer used only for voice communication but are a convenient way of connecting to the Internet and are used for transferring data, exchanging e-mails, and doing small scale business transactions. Next to increase in the adoption of mobile phones comes the growth in the sales of PDAs and pagers. Last year's total PDA sales were estimated to be over 20 million (Sadeh, 2002).

While thee mobiles devices continue to increase taking essential roles in our lives, the wired PC connection to Internet may lose its initial attraction. (At the time of first publication of this paper in 2003, mobile phone penetration was well above home PC usage in Europe and it seems that the trend will continue. At the moment there are more mobile devices connected to the internet than PCs in the world).

The volume of penetration of mobile devices will put severe pressure on m-government implementations. The users will want to have government services (those which are appropriate for mobile technologies) to be delivered and accessible anywhere and anytime. This will lead to mobile government activities reaching a larger base in a more convenient manner.

2.2 The Emergence of Mobile Internet

Conventionally, anywhere – anytime voice communication has been one of the major factors for the growth of mobile phones. Data communications however is now becoming very attractive to many consumers and business users. Japan's NTT DoCoMo created a successful business and technological model for connecting many mobile phone users to the Internet through "i-mode". (Wallace et al, 2002). I-mode was first launched in 1999. In three years more than 43 million subscribers in Japan can access the Internet through their mobile phones. They can exchange e-mails, download ringing tones, access location based information, do simple purchases and read news and other business information using their mobile phones (Supaporn, 2002). Similarly, among other examples "Voda-phone live" in Europe is taking the users to the exciting world of the Internet through their mobile phones. It is expected that by the end of 2004, there will be around 250 Million mobile internet subscribers (The Allied Business Intelligence and Reuters Insight, in Sadeh, 2002).

The technology and the speed of the mobile internet has evolved through various Gs (generations). Initially mobile telephony systems were analog, circuit-switched. Voice links were poor, capacity was low, and security was almost non-existent. Then comes the second-generation (2G) protocols using digital encoding such as GSM and CDMA. These technologies are in use around the world and support high rate of voice but limited data transfers. They offer auxiliary services such as data, fax and SMS. The next generation technologies and protocols, (2.5G) extend 2G systems to provide additional features such as packet-switched connection (GPRS) and enhanced data rates. Third-generation protocols support much higher data rates, and are intended primarily for applications other than voice. 3G applications, at a limited scale, have already started in Japan, Europe, part of Asia/Pacific, and in the US. Full fledged 3G is expected to support bandwidth-hungry applications such as full-motion video, video-conferencing and full Internet access (Sadeh, 2002, Wallace et al, 2002).

Bringing the mobile internet to the mobile devices is not an easy task. These devices have limitations in terms of size (small displays and keyboard) and low memory. Also, the technologies are yet to prove themselves with high speed and smooth transmissions without any disconnection. Various wireless standards and handset compatibilities remain to constitute important challenges to real world business applications and implementations on the mobile internet.

2.3 Mobile Net Applications and Services

NTT DoCoMo's i-mode provides one of the most successful and comprehensive mobile internet applications and services. I-mode is deployed using packet-switched technology allowing users to have an "always on" connection to the internet but paying only for the data that they transfer. Since it is launched in 1999, more than 43 million subscribers of i-mode enjoy various applications and services through DoCoMo's i-mode portal. These services can be categorized into four types: Transaction, information, database and entertainment services. The killer applications for mobile Net in Japan are mostly entertainment type where, for example, users may download screen savers, ring tones and play games. Other services may include browsing information and databases such as news, stock prices, telephone directory and location based dining guides (Supaporn, 2002). One important area that is yet to improve is business applications such as mobile banking, ticket reservations and trading. Apart from Japan, especially in north European countries, mobile net applications are taking a significant place in the lives of many mobile users. Nordea offers one of the first and successful wireless application protocol (WAP) based online banking services. The service allows users to pay bills and check their balances and statements (Sadeh 2002).

Short messaging service (SMS) is by far the killer application of the mobile net (Sadeh, 2002). Almost all mobile phone users use this service. Then comes the entertainment related services such networked games, dating services or downloading ringing tones and screen savers. One of the most needed application area is the business and transactions. There are only a few good examples in banking, travel and location based services such as restaurant guides. Mobile phones are following a trend to become one of the most personalized computing device. One of the sources of the need for personalization comes from the limitations of devices in terms of their size and processing capacity. It s not really possible to present mobile users with abundance of information, nor is it advisable to put the users to inconvenience extensive browsing. Therefore the recent trends in mobile net applications have been tailoring the services to the user's profile. These applications are using as much user's data as possible, to provide location and context aware solutions. They use data regarding who the user is, what is his/her location and other info related to preferences, and aims to suggest what would be relevant to the user. City guides and dining services are typical examples. The more recent applications are aiming discover the context that user is in and then, for example, providing targeted information to the users (Sadeh, 2002).

4. M-government Services

The technology and the services landscape presented above is slowly taking its place in various m-government implementations. Some of the early adopters of m-government services include law enforcements, fire fighting, (Easton, 2002) emergency medical services, education, health and transportation (Zalesak 2002, 2003) (The discussion below is mainly based on (Zalesak 2002, 2003) apart from law enforcement and firefighting sections).

4.1 Law Enforcement

Easton (2002) presents various law enforcement cases from the USA. These cases report various states patrols using mobile devices (Panasonic Toughbooks and PacketCluster

Patrol from Ather systems) connected via a wireless cellular network. The successful examples include Colorado State Patrol, Public safety agency in New York area, the police department in Flint, Michigan and the state patrol in Carmel, Indiana.

In these cases mobile technologies are used to support the activities of state officials who are on the move. These agents can communicate among each other and access various information sources through the wireless network. For example in Colorado the entire state is covered and there is at least 35 percent increase in productivity and thousands of dollars in savings per application. Another benefit includes increase in the speed of processing. For example accident reports processing time is reduced from 6 months to 72 hours (Easton, 2002) where at least two other departments are involved: departments of revenue and transport. The agents are reported to take the wireless system up smoothly since they believe it helps them to do their job better. The cases clearly support the idea that law enforcement applications of m-government lead to cost effective and efficient operations against crime and safety promotions.

4.2 Fire Fighting

The wireless technologies used in firefighting is similar to the way they are used in sales force automation. Basically, mobile technologies allow the fire fighters to know more about critical data related to a fire incident before arriving (Easton, 2002). These data include pre-fire plans, occupancy demographics, building inspection information and relevant information in the surrounding area of the events. The recent efforts are moving towards embedding the smoke alarm systems and sprinklers with wireless sensors which could allow firefighters to know the level of make, a room's temperature and the digital image of the room before they arrive. This would enhance their operations efficiency reducing number of fatalities and improving safety for the firefighters. The wider benefits can be obtained from integrated systems with the police and medical emergency services, resulting in additional savings, efficiencies and community protection.

4.3 M-Government and Education System

Internet and mobile phones play a very important role for an integrated education system, as they provide instant communication among parents, students and schools. Parents can receive frequent updates on academic performance of their children, and sometimes, instant notifications if their children are late or missing a class. This instant communication between parents and schools is highly appreciated by the families especially if both parents are working. Timely communication among educators, parents, and students can prevent academic failure and serious disciplinary actions.

As for the students in higher education, mobile services may provide an opportunity to send and receive announcements on emergencies and public safety, class schedule updates, campus events, traffic and weather conditions, office hours, campus resources available, and exam results. This can help students efficiently utilize wireless devices and note books in a technologically improved academic environment to better inseminate knowledge.

4.4 M-Government and Health Care System

The primary aim of healthcare institutions is to improve the effectiveness of care services but at the same time to reduce the costs. Handheld wireless applications can enable doctors, nurses and other health care professionals to gain access the right information at the right time to prescribe the proper treatment. In addition to saving time for intervention and prevention, using mobile devices can offer great benefits and efficiency with:

- Access to patient records;
- Finding patient's HMO and PCP;
- Access to lab test results;
- Requests for urgent blood donations;
- Access to latest drug reference databases;
- Sending patients' data for a second opinion ;
- Electronic billing for in-home health care workers.

4.5 M-Government and Transportation

Although there are limited mobile applications for the transportation industry, the major companies in the industry are increasingly providing crucial services for road safety and transportation optimization.

Mobil and Interactive transportation routing and scheduling programs can determine the transportation eligibility and establish optimal routes and schedules consistent with regional, national and global policies and resources. Transportation eligibility can be based on constraints such as time and distances, and vehicle capacities. Routes can be formulated for multiple trips in consideration of keeping number of vehicles as low as possible. Mobil devices increase the control to achieve maximum fleet efficiency through route and schedule optimization.

Mobile devices can easily transmit changes in transportation conditions and logistics. The graphic functions of mobile devices can produce computer-generated maps, flight routes, stop locations for delivery, distribution and maintenance. Color-coded display can show speed limits, street names, hundred block addresses and hazardous conditions, if any. General Motors has a system that informs drivers of any potential hazard within 15-mile radius of their location. Wireless technology can be a life saving tool in placing or responding any stress call.

4.6 M-Government and M-Democracy

What may facilitate the participation of citizens in overall government affairs? M-Democracy gives citizens two great opportunities to:
-   Express their opinions directly to the government officials,
-   Monitor the representatives under close control.

How important it is for the government officials surrounded by advisers and assistants to know the authentic opinions and changing expectations of people?
-   M-democracy allows the government to receive feed back directly from public.

- Wireless technology can help through virtual referendums. Governments make forms and publications available online to increase citizens' participation and ask for their opinions. A proposition for a new law or an amendment can be posted on a web site. People with comments, suggestions and questions can send their comments via internet and mobile phones.

Some people may be reluctant to send comments by using a mobile phone because their number is visible at the other end. However, various technical solutions are available to protect privacy. Some countries such as UK and Czech Republic have tried voting via mobile phones. Major concerns were:

- Lack of knowledge about mobile phones;
- Lack of confidence in new technology (many people had fear of missing to vote);
- Cost of sending a vote thru a mobile device;
- Preferences regarding use of SMS messages;
- Fraud, such as a selling out a vote.

5. Challenges for M-government

Every progress has challenges. Implementing m-government will also bring a series of challenges. Some of the typical challenges for e-government are naturally shared by the m-government efforts. Lanwin (2002) states some of these challenges. Among them, we will visit those which are most relevant to m-government including infrastructure development, privacy and security, legal issues, mobile penetration rate and accessibility, compatibility.

- Infrastructure development: For m-government to flourish, the information technology infrastructure must be present. This infrastructure is both physical and 'soft'. The physical infrastructure refers to the technology, equipment, and network required to implement m-government.

  No less important are soft infrastructures such as institutional arrangements, and software that make m-government transactions possible. Even though m-government is in its initial stage, various software are available for m-government services. PacketWriter, Pocket Blue, and Pocket Rescue are a few examples of m-government soft ware developed by Aether systems (for more information, please visit

http://www.aethersystems.com/webfiles/industries/govern ment/#roi).

- Payment infrastructures: are also vital to the success of m-government. A very first obstacle for consumers to buy online is a feeling of mistrust in sending their credit card information over the mobile phone or the Internet. In developing countries, though, another problem precedes that: low credit card penetration. The number of persons with credit cards is too small in comparison to the number of potential users for m-government transactions.

- Privacy and security: are the most significant concerns citizens have about m-government. The general fear is that their mobile phone numbers will be traced, when they send their opinions and inquiries to the government. The government must overcome the mistrust, and assure mobile users that people's privacy is protected and the information will not be sold to third parties.

Although encryption of SMS messages is relatively safe, mobile phone numbers and mobile devices are relatively easy to be hacked. Wireless networks are vulnerable because they use public airwaves to send signals. Because of interception in all traffic on the Internet, there is a big chance for outsiders to attack on wireless networks to steal important information and temper with documents and files. Therefore in the planning stage of the m-government project, privacy and security issues should be considered so that developers will be able to select appropriate mobile devices.

- Accessibility: The success of mobile government will depend on largely the number of its users: the citizens. But socioeconomic factors such as income, education level, gender, age, handicap, language differences and regional discrepancies will affect the citizens' attitude towards mobile government. In order to increase citizen participation and provide citizen-oriented services, governments need to offer easy access to m-government information in alternative forms, possibly, using video and voice communications.

- Legal issues: Many countries around the world have not yet adopted the Law of Fair Information Practices, which spells out the rights of data subjects (citizens) and the responsibilities of the data holders (government). In some cases the law does not recognize mobile documents and transactions. There is no clear legal status for government's online publications, no regulations and laws for online fillings, online signings, and on online taxable transactions.

- Compatibility: One of the technical difficulties might arise from compatibility of the mobile systems with the existing e-government systems. This may get even more serious in the cases of government offices having legacy systems which may not be easy to integrate both in terms of functionalities and data administration.

6. Discussions and Conclusions

The recent developments in business models, services and technologies of the WWW and Internet created new dimensions on the interactivity, mobility and intelligence of the web based solutions. As e-business is evolving towards m-business, e-government seems to follow the trend with a few but significant mobile government (m-government) applications. Millions of mobile phone users, equipped with Internet connections, will put severe pressure on the government to extend appropriate e-government services into the mobile platform. It is now inevitable for e-government professionals, practitioners, and researchers to acquire necessary skills to face the new move towards m-government.
This paper aimed to provide an overview of developments on the

mobile internet technologies and services, and tied them to the existing and future m-government applications and government business models.

M-government is building upon e-government efforts, and there are basically two important issues related to the transition from and the relationship between e-government to m-government:

- *M-government is inevitable.* The major forces influencing m-government adoption include: (a) current technological advances in the areas of wireless World Wide Web and the Internet, (b) benefits to be gained from value added business models stemming from these developments, and (c) the citizen's rising expectations for a better and convenient government services.

- *M-government will be complimentary to e-government.* We have demonstrated various services some of which are replications of e-government services on the mobile platforms. However, the real value of m-government efforts come to surface with those services and applications which are only possible using wireless and mobile infrastructure.

Earlier in the paper we have presented various technological issues as driving forces for m-government. These forces will put severe influence on the new and existing e-government efforts to move towards mobile applications. Some the forces presented include

a) increasing mobile infrastructure and mobile device penetration in Europe and in the World,
b) evolution of mobile internet technologies, standards and protocols towards faster and more sophisticated applications, and
c) adoption of mobile internet applications and services by individuals and businesses.

We have also presented that there already exist various m-government applications and business models in the areas of law enforcement, education, transport, health and firefighting. M-government business models will typically follow an enhanced version of e-government models (Abramson and Means, 2001) where appropriate. We will see applications enabling governments to perform better

a) in serving the citizens using mobile information and communication models;
b) in doing business with the citizens and other government and business organizations using mobile transactions models;
c) in integrating various government units and officials through mobile portals; and
d) in promoting active participation in the government affairs establishing m-democracy models.

There are various challenges to adapting to coming age of M-government revolution such as:

- Developing wireless and mobile networks and related infrastructure
- Promoting mobile penetration and increasing accessibility
- Dealing with an extremely difficult task of protecting privacy and providing security for the data and interactions
- Regulating and developing legal aspects of mobile applications and use of the services.

The existing technological foundations, applications and services support the idea that m-government will be a significant part of e-government efforts. The policy makers and IT professionals need get ready to embrace these developments and participate in the ways to enhance e-government activities through m-government.

References:

Abramson, Mark and Means, E. Grady (Editors), (2001), *E-government 2001*, Rowman and Littlefield Publishers, Inc., New York.

Easton, Jaclyn, (2002), *Going Wireless: transform your business with wireless mobile technology*, HarperCollins, USA (pp. 187-196)

Holmes. D (2001), *eGov: eBusiness Strategies for Government*, Nicolas Brealey.

Lanwin, Bruno, (2002) A Project of Info Dev and The Center for Democracy & Technology: The E-government handbook for developing countries. [online] http://www.cdt.org/egov/handbook/2002-11-14egovhandbook.pdf

Sadeh, Norman, (2002), *M-Commerce: Technologies, Services and Business Models*,   John Wiley and Sons, Inc, Canada and USA.

Supaporn, W. (2002), Exporting I-mode, Unpublished Master's Thesis, e-Business Management, International University of Japan.

Wallace Paul (et al), (2002), I-mode developer's Guide, Addison Wesley, Pearson Education

Zalesak, Michal, Series of articles on m-government at the europemedia.net:
(a) 16/01/2003 Part I: M-Government: more than a mobilised government

http://www.europemedia.net/shownews.asp?ArticleID=14482
(b) 17/01/2003 M-Government: more than a mobilised government, Part II

http://www.europemedia.net/shownews.asp?ArticleID=14495

(c) 30/07/2002 <u>The future of m-government</u>

>http://www.europemedia.net/shownews.asp?ArticleID=11768

(d) 31/07/2002 <u>The future of m-government: Part II</u>

>http://www.europemedia.net/shownews.asp?ArticleID=11824

(e) 07/08/2002 <u>The future of m-government: Part III</u>

>http://www.europemedia.net/shownews.asp?ArticleID=11924

ABOUT THE AUTHORS

Both authors are active members of the mobileGov UK providing consultancy services to governments and other relevant business organizations for designing and implementing strategic mobile government.

mobileGov UK is the world leading consultancy, training and education company. Registered in England and Wales.

For all enquiries please write to ik@mgovernment.net or visit www.mgovernment.net